THE WORSHIP CHRONICLES

JOSE SANTIAGO

PUBLISHING

CONTENTS

DEDICATION

First and foremost, I want to dedicate this book to the only One who gave me the strength to pull through when I had given up hope. To the one who covers, protects, and watches over me daily, giving me the wisdom and understanding to write this book: My Lord and Savior, Jesus Christ. Without Him, this book would not be possible. To Him be all the glory, honor, and praise forever and ever. Amen!

Secondly, I dedicate this book to my wonderful parents. I thank God for gifting me with such wonderful and amazing parents who taught me what it meant to fear the Lord and to serve Him. I thank God for my father, who served as an example of what worship looked like in a person, and my mother, who showed me what an intercessor looked like. I love you both so much!

Last but certainly not least, not by a long shot, I want to dedicate this book to my lovely, beautiful, and amazing wife: a true gem the Lord gave me. Babe, I love you with all my heart and I thank you for pushing me and for believing in me. Thank you so much for your patience and your prayers. God knows how much I needed you. Besides my salvation, you are the best thing that has ever happened to me! Love you forever and always!

FOREWORD

By: Alba Gonzalez

Truly, the depths and profundity of worship can only be known through personal experience and cannot completely be expressed with words. This topic of "praise and worship" is one that is very often spoken about, yet very seldom understood by people. However, these "Worship Chronicles" seek to stir up in the reader that desperate desire to dive deeper into worship where, through personal application and expression, the reader understands it for him/herself. In my experience as a worship leader, I have had to learn how to both maintain a personal life of intimate worship and, also, express outward praise to lead the congregation to deeper worship. The relationship between worship and praise is a beautiful one.

What begins as "praise," the outward expression or acknowledgment of God's righteousness, mercy, or love can then turn into "worship," which comes from your spirit and is a deep surrender to the Holy Spirit. That moment of worship in spirit and truth then turns into a journey, where the Spirit Himself overtakes you and moves you to utter the words, songs, or melodies that will please the Father and cause heaven to open for you. This is the secret the Lord has taught me over the years to keep me close to His heart. I learned that there is a special intimacy with God available to us that we cannot attain through any other means but through praise and worship. Whether through a joyful, outward expression of praise or through a quiet, reverent acknowledgement of His presence, the posture of worship joins you to the Father and opens the heavens! I can personally testify that this "secret" is true, as it has been my success in everything I've done and has been the one thing to carry me through trials. I can remember moments of deep despair in my own life where I had no more words to pray and no willpower left to even pick up my Bible. At times, all I've had left was a "...but I worship You" or a "my soul cries out to You"; an "I want to see Your face" and a "free my soul from its prison so that I may worship You!" It would be in those moments that His heart would pour out into my heart and His glory would overshadow all else. Then all that would be left would be Him and I. And when it was just Him and I (like Paul teaches us in 2 Corinthians 3:18), with an unveiled face, I could behold His glory and be transformed into His image.

It would be during these moments that God would teach me about the secret of worship. Once the Lord had revealed to me the power of praise and worship, He moved me to share it with others. Now as I lead my church and my worship team, I see how in them, the Spirit of God moves freely and powerfully through worship. I remember a specific instance when we had held a leadership meeting at church and a few differences of opinions and doctrine had come up, and some strong words were said by a few people. This had taken place right before our service was about to begin. After I had prayed and gotten up to the altar to begin the service, I looked into the crowd and saw the faces of the people who had been upset. I could clearly see their discomfort and the feeling of division was tangible.

However, though, as the service began and the worship progressed, the Spirit of God took over! And as He moved, I opened my eyes and saw each person engaged in true worship, with all the attention turned to praising Jesus! Their troubles had dissipated and their differences were set aside. At that moment, I realized even more so just how important worship truly was. Worship not only impacts you personally, directly and individually, but it also unites us all back to our main purpose which is exalting Christ. Once again, I had seen the importance of the secret of worship. Now this secret has been forgotten by so many congregations, and it has dimmed the light of the church and stunned its power. If we come back to the heart of worship, though, in our intimacy and within our congregations, we will become aligned to what the Holy Spirit wants to do. I believe God is calling the church to a great revival of true worship that will stir up the Father's heart for an outpouring over His church, and so I know this book will be essential for those who want to be a part of the revival! Read this book and hold it near to your heart, for these Worship Chronicles hold invaluable information for those true worshippers that will be pertinent in these times.

1

GROWING UP IN CHURCH

"Train up a child in the way he should go; even when he is old, he will not depart from it."

— PROVERBS 22:6

It's Sunday morning around eight a.m. The house was buzzing while my parents were running back and forth, getting everything ready for what was sure to be a very long day. I still remember the sound of my parents yelling, "EMANUEL Y JOSE! DESPIERTEN, VAMOS A ESTAR TARDE" which was basically Spanish for "you and your brother better wake up before we come in there and give you something to cry about." Very, and I mean VERY, reluctantly did we get up out of bed. Between you and me, I dreaded Sundays. The day seemed to drag on because our local church had Sunday school from ten a.m. until noon. Then we would go back home, rest for a short while, and then had to be back at five p.m. for the church's night service.

You might be thinking, *that's not so bad* except my father was part of the worship team and usually after Sunday school ended, he had to stay for at least an hour after to rehearse the worship set for that night. OH, and we lived about twenty to thirty minutes away. So, let's do some math. Sunday school ended at noon. By the time everyone but the worship team left, it was around 12:30 p.m. They rehearsed for about an hour so by the time they finished, it was about 1:30-1:45 p.m. Add a half hour until we get home, it was around two p.m. When we got home, we could leave no later than four p.m. since my dad had to be back at church early so that left us about two hours to rest, eat, change, and be on our way. TWO HOURS! By this point, I was thinking, "Jesus, take the wheel."

Now, we grew up Pentecostal. Our church was a church that believed in speaking in tongues, dancing in the Spirit, casting out demons, laying hands on the sick, and praying for miracles...which basically meant that our service had a start time but not an end time. Some days, service would end around 7:30-8 p.m. and other days, it would end well after ten p.m. No, I'm not exaggerating. This was especially true when the church would hold concerts, revivals, and church anniversaries. I distinctly remember how an evangelist by the name of Rafael Sotomayor would come once a year to preach for the church's annual three-day revival. The minute they would mention his name and announce that he was coming, I would deeply sigh and throw a fit because I knew, that weekend, it meant we were going to be in church practically non-stop.

Besides being part of the worship team, my parents were the directors of the home group discipleship program, or "celulas" as they were called. Once a week, they would go to one of the church family's home and would basically have a little service at their house. Besides that, my father was also the vice president of the men's ministry and was one of the church deacons, while my mother also was the vice president of the women's ministry.

Because a lot of people knew of my father and his voice, my parents would get invited either to preach and/or sing at different churches. Around that same time, my brother and I learned how to play the drums so we would often be a part of worship.

So, yeah, all of this is to truly engrain in your brain the fact that I REALLY grew up IN church. I wasn't a bi-weekly visitor or distant bystander. I was in the middle of the "party" itself, week in and week out. I got to see the good, the bad, and the ugly of growing up as a preachers/worshiper's kid.

Not everything that glitters is gold, however, and no one knows what's in the pot except the one that is stirring it. From the outside looking in, we seemed like the perfect "ministry family." Yet, all the time I spent in church created in me a resentment that slowly turned into full-blown rebellion. When I was eleven, my parents moved us from Connecticut to Florida in order to pursue the calling of God over their lives. It was during this time that my "church rebellion" began. My parents can testify that when they would try to wake me up on a Sunday morning to get ready for church, I would throw the worst fits, slamming doors and throwing whatever I could get my hands on because I absolutely refused to go. Of course, they would still force me, but I did everything in my power to make it difficult for them.

To be fair, however, it wasn't easy for a kid/pre-teen to be raised Pentecostal. The way my parents initially raised my older brother and I was the same way they were brought up in their church in Puerto Rico. In the Hispanic community, we call it being "raja tabla" or "table breaker," which is referring to people being overly religious or people who follow an extremely strict form of Christianity. They were basically taught that everything was a sin. Women wearing pants was a sin; going to the movies was a sin; going to the beach; having friends sleeping over; men having beards, etc. Oh, and let's not forget the thought that if a preacher didn't wear a suit and tie to preach, he wasn't anointed. So, even though my parents weren't extreme, they were still strict, which just fueled my rebellion because I felt I couldn't do anything.

Around eighth or ninth grade, I began learning how to play guitar and became obsessed with heavy metal. I still remember my mother's reaction when my friend Dillon told her we were going to start a rock band called "Seventh Day South"! Her eyes opened really big and she just looked at me like "No, the heck you're not." Needless to say, I was never in a rock band thanks to Momma, which, again, made me more and more rebellious.

It got so bad that my parents basically said, "God, You deal with him," because they could no longer afford to have shouting matches at home with me and then go to an altar to worship as if everything was ok. So, they just left me in God's hands and let His will be done in my life. They stopped forcing me to go to church (most of the time) and simply let me be. Now, let me take a moment here and speak to every mother and father out there that are dealing with children that are not serving the Lord right now.

All the time you spent teaching your children the ways of God was not in vain. Every time you went into their room in the middle of the night to lay hands on them and cover them in prayer was not pointless. You've done your part. You've loved them and taught them as best as you could. Now, put your faith and trust in God; be at peace and know that God is going to do a mighty work in their lives! Can I get an amen?

Now, even though I didn't realize it at the time, I realize that all my experiences as a boy practically living in church was God's way of preparing me for what He is doing in my life today. Every service, every revival, every opportunity I've had to witness my father sing and my mother minister were just "seeds" deposited in my spirit coming to fruition many years later.

2

FROM REBEL TO PROPHET

"Before I formed you in the womb, I knew you, and before you were born, I consecrated you; I appointed you a prophet to the nations."

— JEREMIAH 1:5

Right around my tenth grade year, I started going back to church. I would often accompany my mother to the Tuesday night prayer service, though I kept to myself and didn't really say or do anything besides sit near the back and listen. I still was living my rebellious life but I, for one reason or another, began to enjoy being at church again. Fast forward a few months later and the church had its monthly youth service. Now, for those of you who didn't grow up in a traditional Hispanic Pentecostal church as I did, let me fill you in.

Sundays were the main evangelistic-style service while Tuesdays were either prayer service or Bible study. Thursday nights, however, was when each ministry within the church would alternate overseeing the service. That means every department would be in charge once a month. The men's ministry oversaw one Thursday, then the women's ministry, then the children's ministry and, finally, the youth ministry. Most Hispanic churches still organize their services in this manner even now.

I was seated in the second row from the front, in the last seat on the lefthand side of the church. Service had already ended, and I believe one of the youth leaders was giving the final announcements before dismissing the service. As I sat there, I distinctly remember the following thought entering my mind: "You can't run away from your calling forever."

I didn't move; I didn't say a word; it was almost as if I was paralyzed. "You can't run away from your calling forever." Nobody came up to me and laid hands on me; no one prophesied to me; no one did anything. The service was already over, and I was sitting by myself in the pew! Yet that thought was penetrating every fiber of my being. It brought back to memory when the Lord spoke to me for the first time, around three years prior, when I was twelve years old.

Our youth pastors at the time had invited a pastor from Tampa, Florida to come minister at our youth service. During the altar call, literally every single one of the youths from our church came forward to receive prayer. And by the way, we had a big youth group and I was all the way on the righthand side of the altar. This meant that I was going to be one of the last people the preacher was going to pray for. Suddenly, I begin to tremble and fight back tears. But one thing I have learned is that you cannot resist the presence of God.

I began to weep but I tried to hide my tears. However, seemingly out of nowhere, I felt these very soft hands touch my back and heard this soothing, yet authoritative, voice speak from behind me. It was the preacher's wife. She came up to me, speaking in tongues, and I completely lost it. The few tears I was trying to hold back seemingly turned into rivers coming from my eyes. The presence of God became so overwhelming, she literally had to hold me up because I could barely stand. I'm reminded of the verse in Psalm 114, where it states that the earth trembles at the presence of God. And, if the earth trembles, imagine us.

Anyway, the preacher's wife leaned into my ear and the Lord began to use this lady, who I'd never seen before, to tell me everything He was going to do in my life: everything from my calling to the ministry He had for me to the gifts He gave me. It seemed as if she ministered to me for AT LEAST a half hour. And then three years later, I was sitting down in church and the Lord was reminding me once again that there was a calling over my life that I couldn't run from.

So, I summoned all the courage and bravery that was in my scrawny, little teenage body and after the service was dismissed, I walked over to our youth pastors and this was the conversation that followed: Me: "Hey... I have a question...do you guys have anyone that is preaching for next youth service?" Youth pastors: "Yeah, we have so-and-so who is going to preach... why?" Me: "Oh. Because I was going to ask if maybe I could preach..." Youth pastors: "You want to preach?! Well, like I said, so-and-so is going to preach but the youth service after next we don't have anyone. Would you like to preach on that one?" Me: "Yeah, for sure!"

Two months passed by in what seemed like an instant. The service was announced, and I spend the day fasting, praying, and being more nervous than I had ever been before (or after). August 9, 2010, 7:30pm: Let me tell you I was shaking as if there was a massive earthquake happening and it was not due to the anointing! I was dreading the moment when the pastor was going to call my name. And before I knew it, she grabbed the microphone and said, "Vamos a tener a nuestro hermano Jose

Santiago con la palabra," which means "Let's have our brother Jose Santiago come forward bring the word."

The next twenty to thirty minutes seemed almost like a blur. I clearly remember preaching about when God humbled Kind Nebuchadnezzar for seven years. The message was about humbling oneself before God but that's pretty much what I remember from the message itself. What followed though was a clear confirmation of what I was meant to do for the rest of my life. That night, I had my friend Jean translating for me. Once the message ended, I made the altar call and asked if there was anyone that wanted to pass forward and humble themselves before God. I closed my eyes, quietly thanked God, and then turned to give my friend Jean a hug and tell him, "Thank you." However, I didn't expect what I was about to witness next.

I had almost forgotten I had made the altar call, so when I looked up, I was shocked! I didn't see almost anyone sitting in the congregation, except maybe two or three people. Now, growing up in a Pentecostal church, all you would hear is "CRISTO VIENE!" meaning "Christ is coming back." This, of course, is referring to the sudden rapture of the church, as was, and is, so famously preached, "He's coming back in the blink of an eye and if you are not ready, you will be left behind!" So, my thought was, "Oh my God. The rapture happened and I stayed!" I know, don't laugh. Not funny! However, that wasn't the case, and I began to hear people praying behind me.

When I turned around, I saw the entire congregation on their knees on the altar! Each of them was responding to the Word from God and humbling themselves before His presence. So, what did I do? I spent a good amount of time individually praying for every person that was on the altar. Among the people that were at the altar was my father and my pastor. For me, that was a complete surprise. I had witnessed my father minister through worship since I was a child, and I heard my pastor preach sermon after sermon, yet now it was my turn to minister to them! Me!

I didn't hear the Lord audibly speak that night but to me, He was abundantly clear. "I have called you for such a time as this to deliver My Word throughout the nations. Do not be afraid for I am with you." It reminds me of when God called the prophet Jeremiah yet Jeremiah though he was too young to be used by God.

Then I said, "Ah, Lord GOD! Behold, [1]I do not know how to speak, [m]for I am only a youth." But the LORD said to me, "Do not say, 'I am only a youth'; for to all to whom I send you, you shall go, and [n]whatever I command you, you shall speak."

— JEREMIAH 1:6

There I was, a fifteen-year-old kid who used to make his parents' lives impossible, yet through the grace and mercy of God, that same kid has now become a preacher. I had no idea exactly what was coming next. All I knew is that I had a word from God and a passion to preach His Word.

3

CREATED FOR A PURPOSE

"Oh come, let us sing to the Lord; let us make a joyful noise to the rock of our salvation! Let us come into his presence with thanksgiving; let us make a joyful noise to him with songs of praise! For the Lord is a great God, and a great King above all gods. In his hand are the depths of the earth; the heights of the mountains are his also. The sea is his, for he made it, and his hands formed the dry land. Oh come, let us worship and bow down; let us kneel before the Lord, our Maker! For he is our God, and we are the people of his pasture, and the sheep of his hand."

— PSALM 95:1-7

A question we have all asked ourselves is "Why am I here?" From our childhoods, past our adolescent years, and through adulthood, each of us has gone back and forth trying to figure out that age-old question. Countless books and articles have been written trying to decipher the mystery of the human existence. Every sage, every wise man, every spiritual leader, scientist, philosopher, shaman, politician, etc., has tried to understand how we came to be and why we exist in the first place. Some believe we exist out of pure, random coincidence; that everything came from an infinitesimal point, which exploded and over billions upon billions of years creating the fundamental building blocks of life... again, all by pure chance. Some believe that we are descendants from a species of primate, while others believe we were created by a multitude of different celestial beings or "gods." Every culture and every religion have its own version of the creation story, each with its own explanation of our existence.

When we open the Word to the book of Genesis, we read the following verse:

"In the beginning, God created the heavens and the earth."

— *GENESIS 1:1*

I would like to take a minute and speak about the first four words of that verse: "In the beginning, God..." One thing that should be abundantly clear is the only thing that has been, and always will be, eternally self-existent is God Himself.

"...and He is before all things, and in Him all things hold together."

— COLOSSIANS 1:17

> *"Before the mountains were brought forth, or ever you had formed the earth and the world, from everlasting to everlasting you are God."*
>
> — PSALM 90:2

Everything that is seen and unseen is a creation of He who has always existed. Nothing in creation can possibly exist without Him, yet He does not need anything or anyone to exist! He is not governed by time, space, or matter. He is not bound by any of the scientific or governmental laws invented by man. He... is... GOD!

Now, we do not know at what point in time God decided to, basically, create everything. The Bible doesn't give us a date or a time frame to go by. The narrative simply states that creation was made in the span of six days, with God resting on the seventh. As we read further down, two verses capture my attention:

> *Then God said, "Let us make man in our image, after our likeness."*
>
> — *GENESIS 1:26*

> *Then the Lord God formed the man of dust from the ground and breathed into his nostrils the breath of life, and the man became a living soul."*
>
> — *GENESIS 2:7*

The first reason these verses capture my attention is because up until this point in the Bible, everything God created He spoke into existence. God said, "Let there be light" and there was light. God said, "Let there be vegetation and trees and animals" and it was so. I repeat, everything that was created was spoken into existence...except mankind. When God decided to create us, He deemed us important and special enough to not simply "Speak us into existence," but rather He came down, rolled up His sleeves, got in the dirt, and formed us with His own two hands; something He didn't do for anything else! Now, I don't know about you, but that is enough to make me get up and shout! We are God's "Magnum Opus"; we are **His masterpiece!**

The second reason is because the verses show we were made in God's image and likeness. You might be wondering "But what does that even mean? Why does that even matter?" Well, there is a certain being who, according to the book of Isaiah, also wanted to be *"like"* God. But we will dive into that in a later chapter. For now, I want us to fully grasp the fact that we were created by God *with a purpose*. God has a reason for EVERYTHING. We were not created one day simply because God was bored and didn't have anything else to do. God was not looking to simply be entertained. He has a purpose for everything He does.

"declaring the end from the beginning and from ancient times things not yet done, saying, My counsel shall stand, and I will accomplish all my purpose."

— ISAIAH 46:10

I remember some years ago, a pastor who I consider to be like a spiritual father to me, Pastor Rafael "Rafy" Estrada, told me a story that really made me think. He began to tell me how one day he was walking down the street, minding his own business. Out of nowhere, he said he heard the voice of the Spirit tell him, "Go to that lady over there and tell her that I said 'horse.'" He said he stopped what he was doing and said, "You want me to tell her...horse?" and the Lord repeated to him, "Tell her I said 'horse'"

Let me stop here for a second and say I guarantee that every one of us would have questioned God repeatedly. It makes no sense why the Lord would send me to go tell a person, "Hey, the Lord told me to tell you ...'horse.'" It's ludicrous. Preposterous. Insane. Crazy. Loony. It would make me think that the Lord finally went coo-coo for cocoa puffs! Most of us would undoubtedly say, "Nope! Not happening. Nuh-uh. Thanks, but no thanks. I'm good." But again, God doesn't do or say anything unless it served a specific purpose ... and Pastor Rafy knew this.

So even though he had no clue why in the world God was sending him over to this woman to say just one word, Pastor Rafy obeyed. "Excuse me. Sorry to bother you but the Lord told me to tell you, 'Horse'!" I can imagine he was waiting for the woman to laugh in his face and tell him to go away. But he goes on to tell me that almost immediately, the woman burst out in tears, sobbing uncontrollably. She began to tell him how she owned a horse ranch and how she was asking the Lord all these different questions and was waiting for a word from the Lord. Instantly, the word of the Lord came to Pastor Rafy, and he began to prophesy to this woman about everything the Lord was going to do in her life! The woman was filled with strength and direction, all because one man was crazy enough to obey God over a seemingly ridiculous and pointless word. I wonder how many times God has wanted to do something incredible in our lives, and in the lives of those around us, yet because we don't obey the things that seem "pointless," we don't see the hand of God as we should.

Beloved brother and sister in the faith, nothing in your life has happened by pure chance. Nothing that you have ever been through was a coincidence. You weren't born in this time and place out of dumb luck. Your life has been ordained by the Lord from before you were even conceived in your mother's womb! King David said the following sentiment in Psalm 139:16:

"Your eyes saw my unformed substance; in your book were written, every one of them, the days that were formed for me, when as yet there was none of them."

David here lets us know that before he was even born, God had already written down what was going to happen in every single day in his life! God knew beforehand what David's life was going to be like and already had a plan and purpose established for him. And if it was true for David, it is true for every one of us. But even with the different, individual plans God has for us, there is one plan and purpose that goes above and beyond everything else. Let's dig a little deeper.

4

BORN TO WORSHIP

"And Jesus answered him: It is written, you shall worship the Lord your God and Him only shall you serve."

— LUKE 4:8

One of the most famous stories found in the Bible is the story of Jesus and the Samaritan woman. Found in John chapter 4, this beautiful and heartwarming story begins with Jesus, seeing this Samaritan woman was drawing water from a well, asked her for a drink. Her reply, from the outside looking in, was seemingly rude and sarcastic to Him. However, Jews and Samaritans had a long history of feuds and did not get along in the slightest. Plus, she was a woman after all, and women in those days didn't get anywhere near the same treatment and respect women these days do. So, it can be expected that she would be a little on the defensive.

This began a beautiful exchange between the two of them and we are offered a glimpse of what the grace of God looks like.

However, the further down the chapter we read, we notice that the exchange goes from simply asking for water to something much, much deeper.

Our fathers worshipped on this mountain, but you say that in Jerusalem is the place where people ought to worship.

— JOHN 4:20

What began as a conversation that started out because of thirst turned into an issue of worship. Talk about going from 0 to 100 quick! The Samaritan woman believed that worship was something you did at a specific place and time. The Jews worshipped in Jerusalem and the Samaritans worshipped on the mountain they were standing on. Yet Jesus's reply was sure to rock her traditional, religious belief system to its core.

Jesus said to her, "Woman, believe me, the hour is coming when neither on this mountain nor in Jerusalem will you worship the Father."

— JOHN 4:21

Jump down two verses and He continues to say:

But the hour is coming, and is now here, when the true worshipers will worship the Father in spirit and truth, for the Father is seeking such people to worship him.

— *JOHN 4:23*

In the middle of this powerful conversation at the well, Jesus gave this woman a lesson on worship. He began by letting her know that worship is not about the *place* so much as it is about the *heart!* He let her know that God wasn't looking to designate a specific place where one can go to worship. He is looking for people that, **regardless of where they are**, can worship Him from the very depths of their spirit! I don't know about you but that's enough to make me have a praise break all by myself!

It's interesting to note that the Father is "seeking" true worshippers. He is actively searching throughout the earth for those of us who will make the decision to worship Him. Has anyone ever asked themselves why would God seek worshippers when He already has a host of angels in heaven that worship Him? I mean, the Bible clearly states that there are beings around His throne that sing praises continually!

And the four living creatures, each of them with six wings, are full of eyes all around and within, and day and night they never cease to say, "Holy, holy, holy, is the Lord God Almighty, who was and is and is to come!"

— *REVELATION 8:4*

So, if God has a myriad of angelic beings that continually praise and worship Him, why did Jesus tell this Samaritan woman that the Father seeks those who will worship Him? Well, the answer has been right in front of us our entire lives, yet most of us have been too blind to see it. It is the reason why there are so many religions in the world, because mankind was **CREATED TO WORSHIP!!!**

Isaiah 43:21 says:

This people I have formed for Myself; They shall declare My praise.

Isaiah 43:7 says:

everyone who is called by my name, whom I created for my glory, whom I formed and made.

"Whom I created for my glory" or, in other words, "whom I created to glorify (praise, worship, bring honor to) Me." The chief end of man, and I really want this to get deep inside your spirit, is to *worship God* and have *fellowship with Him*! We can try to escape it or deny it all we want but at the end of the day, all of us worship something or someone. It is in our DNA and is in the very fabric that makes us who we are as a species. It is something that is engrained into our souls. We. Were. Made. To. Worship!

You might be asking yourself, "If we were made to worship, why is the Father seeking worshippers if that is what we were created for in the first place?" Good question! And the answer is as follows: Due to Adam and Eve's rebellion in the Garden of

Eden, sin entered the world and shattered that perfect unity between God and man. Sin allowed evil to enter into the heart of man and as mankind began to flourish and spread throughout the earth, man began to abandon their worship of God to worship, instead, many different idols. This is the reason we have Greek, Roman, and Norse mythologies. This is the reason why the Israelites would repeatedly begin to serve the gods of other nations, such as Baal, Ashtoreth, Moloch, and so on. But it doesn't stop there.

Idol worship doesn't have to mean you bowing down in front of a picture on the wall or a statue in your front yard. People worship many things: careers, money, sex, spouses, cars, and so on. In other words, whatever "thing" is number 1 in your life, that is the object of your worship. As we see, mankind is able to *choose* who or what they will worship, so it is a conflict of interest. So, what Jesus was saying in that verse was that the Father is seeking those who will willingly *choose* to worship Him. He is seeking those that will put Him first above their jobs, their families, and yes, even their ministries! For the Father is seeking (actively searching for) worshippers that will worship Him!

This lesson on worship is best shown in Daniel 3. King Nebuchadnezzar ordered a giant 90-foot-tall golden statue to be created. Once it was finished, there was a dedication ceremony and everyone from around the empire was there. The king, however, only had one rule.

> *"You are commanded, O peoples, nations, and languages, that when you hear the sound of the horn, pipe, lyre, trigon, harp, bagpipe, and every kind of music, you are to fall down and **worship** the golden image that King Nebuchadnezzar has set up."*
>
> — *DANIEL 3:4-5*

This was not a suggestion but a command. Everyone within the sound of the instruments were ordered to worship the image. If you did not, there were severe consequences. Verse 6 says the following:

> *"And whoever does not fall down and worship shall immediately be cast into a burning fiery furnace."*

The consequences were severe enough that it would naturally quell any inclination someone might have to resist this command...except three brave, young, Hebrew boys by the names of Shadrach, Meshach, and Abednego. They defiantly opposed this order from the king and refused to bow down to the image. Because of their defiance, they were brought to the king to answer for their rebellion. The Bible states that Nebuchadnezzar was filled with furious rage and demanded to know why they refused to worship the image. Yet the three Hebrews said something we can all learn from and apply:

"O Nebuchadnezzar, we have no need to answer you in this matter. If this be so, our God whom we serve is able to deliver us from the burning fiery furnace, and he will deliver us out of your hand, O king. But if not, be it known to you, O king, that we will not serve your gods or worship the golden image that you have set up."

— *DANIEL 3:16-18*

In other words, the three Hebrews said, "We have already made the choice of who we will worship. Even if you throw us into the fire and even if our God doesn't save us, our decision is final. We will only bow to and worship God!" Now THAT is the kind of worshipper the Father is seeking: Someone who is unwavering in their conviction and their decision to worship Him! Someone that even in the face of certain death, like these three young men, can stand firm and say, "I will only worship God!"

5

THE MEANING OF WORSHIP

"Worship the Lord your God, and His blessing will be on your food and water..."

— EXODUS 23:25

As a preacher in full-time ministry, I have been invited to preach in countless churches. I'm pretty sure that, by now, I've preached at most major Christian denominations and have met a plethora of people. Every church I have been to and every person I have met along the way has their own unique perspective on worship. If I were to ask a hundred people to tell me what worship is, I'm sure I would get a hundred different answers! Yet even with their distinct answers, they all would have one common thread.

Like the Samaritan woman who thought worship was only what happened on the mountain, most people only equate worship as something that is done at the beginning of every Sunday or

Friday service at their local church gathering. They believe worship is simply what happens when the worship team stands on the altar for thirty to forty-five minutes. Although that is part of it, as we will see in a later chapter, it is because of this rudimentary understanding on worship that we tend to miss out on truly developing a deep relationship with God. Let me put it into perspective for you.

For my married folk, I want you to imagine the moment you fell in love with your wife or husband. For my single people, imagine meeting Mr./Mrs. Right. You're casually strolling along when suddenly, your knight-in-shining-armor appears. Or, for the guys, imagine one day just eating your lunch when suddenly that supermodel you've been praying for (can I get an amen?) comes up to you, telling you that her car battery died and she needs a jump. Imagine you wanting to develop a close relationship with that person, yet only speaking to him/her for one hour, once a week.

Imagine trying to get to really know that person and develop a strong bond with them, yet only dedicating that ONE HOUR A WEEK to them. Do you truly think you are going to get very far? Do you truly think you can marry Mr. and Mrs. Right while barely knowing them? For my married couples, how would you have felt if your husband would've proposed to you after spending so little time with you? Pretty sure you would've said no. Not because you didn't think he was good-looking but because you barely know him. Now take that same principle and apply it to your relationship with God. Do you truly think you can develop a strong relationship with God all the while thinking that a thirty-minute worship "session" on Sunday is enough? My point is this: Through a proper understanding of what worship is, we can use it to get closer to God than we have ever been before!

The Bible mentions the word "worship" a total of 188 times and the word "praise" 259 times. Just with those sheer numbers alone, it shows us the importance of worship. So important in fact that when God gave Moses the Ten Commandments, the first two deal exclusively with, you guessed it, ***worship!***

> *"You shall have no other gods before me. You shall not make for yourself a carved image, or any likeness of anything that is in heaven above, or that is in the earth beneath, or that is in the water under the earth. You shall not bow down to them or serve them, for I the LORD your God am a jealous God..."*
>
> — *EXODUS 20: 3-5*

God wanted to truly engrain into the mind of the Israelites, who were recently set free from bondage in Egypt, an idolatrous nation, that above all else, He is demanding their praises and their worship. He didn't want their worship to be split between Himself AND something else. He didn't want a part-time worship. He wanted nothing more than their pure, unadulterated devotion and commitment.

Why was this so important? Well, as stated before, the Israelites had spent over 400 years captive in a nation that worshipped over one thousand "gods." They were no strangers to being surrounded by a people that at one moment worshipped one god and, in the next moment, were offering sacrifices to another. Moreover, the desert area that God brought the Israelites into was also surrounded by many different tribes and nations who also worshipped and served countless "gods." So, in many ways, they had idolatry almost instilled into their minds, and God wanted to break that idolatrous mentality to have them truly understand that He alone was worthy of their worship.

This is critical to point out because Jesus said in Matthew 6:24 that "no one can serve two masters..." because what will happen is that we will love one of them and absolutely despise the other. Throughout the book of Judges and onward, this was a common thread. God commanded the Israelites to only worship Him. They disobeyed and began worshipping other false idols, and the judgement of God came upon them. The story repeated itself over and over again, and it took the Israelites over an entire millennium to grasp the fact that their worship was to be reserved exclusively for God!

Now, according to the dictionary, the word "worship" is defined in three ways:

1. the reverence offered to a divine being.
2. a form of religious practice with creeds and rituals.
3. the extravagant respect or admiration for or devotion to an object.

I want to take a moment here and truly dissect the third definition that is given: "The extravagant respect... or devotion to..." The word "extravagant" means "lacking restraint." For example, a person who is described to have an extravagant lifestyle is someone who knows no limits. They spend insane amounts of money on whatever they want simply because they can. Take Floyd Mayweather, for instance, one of the richest boxers of all time. The other day, he showed up to an interview wearing $22 million dollars' worth of jewelry. I believe he had a watch that cost $17 million and a chain that cost another $5 million. He has many cars, many houses and mansions, etc., so basically he has whatever he wants. That is someone who has an extravagant lifestyle; or better put, a lifestyle without restraint.

So, when we use the word "extravagant" to describe our worship, we are basically saying that our respect, love, and devotion to God must be without restraint. It cannot be held down by our timidity nor by our fear of what others think of us. When it comes to our worship of God, the entire world should be able to see in us the extravagant devotion and admiration we have to our King in every area of our lives!

If there was one man in the Bible who knew what extravagant worship was, it was King David. There is a story found in 2 Samuel 6 and 1 Chronicles 13-16 in which David along with 30,000 men, including the Levitical priests, singers, and musicians, were returning to Jerusalem after going on a trip to Obed-Edom's home to reclaim the arc of the covenant. The text shows us how the entire way back to Jerusalem, David and all who were with him were dancing and rejoicing the whole way there, praising and worshiping the Lord *"with all his might"* (v. 14).

Now, being a king, you would think David had to tone it down and bear some kind of "kingly decency." However, David couldn't have cared any less what anyone thought of him. He wasn't interested in the fact that he was king. He wasn't interested in who was looking at him. He wasn't interested in what anyone said about him. All he cared about in that moment was worshipping and praising with all his might *without restraint!* David's worship was **EXTRAVAGANT!**

So, as you can see, far more than what is done at a church service, *worship* entails that our entire lives manifest the full-on, unrestrained devotion, respect, admiration, and surrender to our Lord Jesus Christ! It is what we do from the moment we arise in the morning to the last thing we do when we are about to fall asleep. When the Father looks down from heaven, seeking worshippers, He is seeking those of us who, like David, will forget about who is watching and who will say what, put everything in second place, and enthrone Him as first in every area of our lives!

We've covered quite a bit of ground so far but there is still so much more to unpack!

This is still the tip of the iceberg, so let's continue.

6

WORSHIP AS A SACRIFICE
HEBREWS 13:15

"Through him then let us continually offer up a sacrifice of praise to God, that is, the fruit of lips that acknowledge his name."

Before I became a preacher, traveling all over spreading the gospel, I was a very ambitious young boy. I had a fascination with astronomy and my goal in life was to be two things: a pilot and an astronaut. I've watched every astronaut movie and witnessed the live television feed of almost every space shuttle launch and landing growing up. I read every book and every article I could get my hands on that had anything to do with space, the planets, the stars, scientific advancements, and so on. Not only that, but by the time I got to high school, I was enrolled in our school's Army JROTC program and acted as if I was already in the military! Imagine seeing a skinny, 5 foot 2 fourteen or fifteen-year-old walking around in an old army camo uniform, barking orders at other kids my age. Now that was a sight to behold!

Overly ambitious, head full of fantasies, a dreamer at heart, I was a boy on a mission. My mother once told me that I was a boy that seemed bent on conquering the world! Yet by the time I was sixteen, with God calling me to preach, I had a choice to make. It was either I continue down the path that I was going and maybe one day work for NASA, join the military or become a pilot for a famous airline company: Or, I leave those earthly ambitions to follow the call of God over my life.

I'm sure many of you can relate. Most of us who have been called into ministry in whatever capacity have a story like mine. You thought you had your entire life planned out and here comes God basically wrecking your plans, calling you to do something in which, more often than not, you don't want to do... AT ALL! See, most people have a difficult time wrapping their heads around the fact that one of the fundamental aspects of a Christian life, especially that of a minister, is a life of *self-denial*. That is why in Matthew 16:24, Jesus tells His disciples that if anyone wants to follow Him, they must *deny* themselves and take up their cross, which is a symbol of *sacrifice*.

You can't follow Jesus AND follow the roadmap you have created for yourself. You cannot follow Jesus AND your own selfish ambitions. It doesn't work that way. Hence why when the disciples asked Jesus to teach them to pray, Jesus laid out a prayer "blueprint" if you will, on how to do just that. In one part of the prayer, He said the following:

"*Thy kingdom come, Thy **will** be done in earth, as it is in heaven.*"

— *MATTHEW 6:10*

Of all the different things Jesus could have included in the prayer "blueprint," He specifically taught them to pray for God's will to be done. In a time in which most people simply pray, thinking of God as a genie that will grant them their every desire, be the one that says "God, You know I want all this but, above it all, I want Your will to be done in my life and in the lives of those around me." How many can just take a second and pray that with me today? Say with me: "God, let Your will be done!"

Why is this so important to know? Remember how in the last chapter, we learned that to truly worship, we must have an extreme devotion to our God? Well, part of that extreme, with-out-restraint devotion and admiration is being willing to *sacrifice* the things in our lives that we value the most. Let me break it down for you.

One of the most famous stories we find in the Bible is the story of the father of our faith, Abraham, and his son Isaac. Those of you familiar with this story will recall how Abraham and his wife Sarah couldn't have children. That is until one day God showed up (quite literally) and promised them a son, and promised Abraham that his descendance would be as numerous as the stars in the sky and the sand on the beach. Long story short, when Abraham was a hundred years old and Sarah was ninety, they received what God had promised them: a beautiful, baby boy!

To put things into perspective, there are many people who waited a very long time to have children. Some people didn't have children until their thirties, forties or even, in some rare instances, their fifties! Some people waited by personal choice but, more often than not, it was due to some sort of illness or infertility. A person who is close to me had a similar predica-ment. She had ovarian cysts and doctors continually told her it was almost impossible for her to ever have children. She would often try to get pregnant but to no avail. Often, the pain she felt was unbearable and she would weep at the prospect of seeing all her friends and families have their own children except for her.

But see, what I love about God is that He always has the last word. Man can declare one thing, but God has the power to change every diagnostic in the blink of an eye! Somebody shout "Hallelujah" at this! After much trying, she and her husband decided to put this situation into the Lord's hands. And lo and behold, before she knew it, she was pregnant with the cutest, little baby girl I've ever laid my eyes on. I vividly remember when her husband called from the hospital after the baby was born. He turned on his video camera so I can see the wife holding the baby. She was fighting back tears and stared so intently into her newborn child. It was as if to say, "Mommy waited all her life to have you. I will never let you go."

The love she had for her baby could be felt even through the video call. They were miles and miles away from where I was, yet the love that oozed from the mother was almost palpable! Now, this was a woman who was in her thirties. Imagine waiting until you are a hundred years old to hold in your hands the child that God has promised you! Can you imagine how you would react when you held that child in your arms after waiting an entire *century!?* I guarantee you that even to just put the baby down in the crib, it would be a challenge! So, Abraham and Sarah raised Isaac with all the love they could muster. They protected him more than anything and watched over him like nobody's business.

Yet on one fateful day, God spoke to Abraham and told him this:

> *"Take your son, your only son Isaac, whom you love, and go to the land of Moriah, and offer him there as a burnt offering on one of the mountains of which I shall tell you."*
>
> — GENESIS 22:2

God told Abraham to take the son that he loved, the son that God gave to him, the son he waited a hundred years for, to offer him up... as a sacrifice. I can't begin to imagine the thoughts that went through Abraham's head, and the emotions that raged within His heart, at the news. *How could God tell him to sacrifice the very son whom He had promised him? Why is this even necessary?* He waited his whole life for Isaac, and now he had to kill the very son that he loved!

But being the obedient man that he was, Abraham listened to the voice of God. He took Isaac, along with two servants, and headed on a three-day journey to Mount Moriah. Once there, He told his two servants some of the most profound words found in all of Scripture.

> *"Stay here with the donkey; I and the boy will go over there and worship..."*
>
> — *GENESIS 22:5*

This is something that, even to this day, blows my mind. Abraham was about to climb this mountain to sacrifice his son, yet he told his two servants that he was going to go *worship*. How is it that what God calls **sacrifice**, Abraham calls **worship**? Could it be possible that part of that extravagant devotion to

God means having to sometimes sacrifice that which we love most? Could it be possible that to truly worship God, we must be willing to sacrifice our "Isaac"?

When we read the book of Romans, we find the apostle Paul talk about this very thing in chapter 12 when he tells us to present our bodies as a *"living sacrifice,"* which is our **"spiritual worship."** See, when God requires you to give something up, regardless of what it might be, and you are willing to give it up, you are worshipping. Whenever you sacrifice your desires, your dreams, your ambitions to follow God's plan for your life, you are worshipping. Whenever you choose God over everything the world has to offer, you...are...worshipping! Because more than being about how good you sing, worship is about offering God a sacrifice!

7

EXPRESSIONS OF WORSHIP

"I will bless the LORD at all times: his praise shall continually be in my mouth."

— PSALM 34:1

One of the things I love most about God, outside of the fact that He sent His only Son to die in our place (can I get an amen?), is the fact that God is extremely creative and manifests His glory in various ways. If you don't believe me, then I challenge you to wake up just before sunrise. Make yourself a nice cup of coffee, or if you are like me, go to the nearest 7/11 and get a 16-ounce cup of Cuban coffee with milk. Believe me, you don't know what good coffee is until you've had Cuban coffee.

I digress. The point is, grab your coffee, your tea, whatever your early morning drink of choice is and go outside and just...wait. Look up to the sky and watch the sun rise slowly over the horizon. Listen to the birds sing and let the cool, early morning breeze caress your face. What you are experiencing and seeing is a manifestation of God's glory. Whenever it rains and a rainbow forms, we are not seeing the symbol for the LGBTQ community; we are seeing the promise and glory of God made manifest in the sky. When NASA release new images of distant stars, planets, galaxies, comets, and so forth, we are seeing the workmanship and creativity of God. Psalm 19:1 tells us that *"The heavens (the sun, moon, stars, clouds, etc.) declare the glory of God and the firmament declares His handiwork."*

Genesis chapter 1 paints a clear picture of creation and, as we know, in each of the first six days, God creates something different. He is the original Picasso; the original Michelangelo, and the universe is His Sistine Chapel. Now, as human beings created in the image and likeness of God, we can attribute our creativity to Him. So, it would only make sense that our worship toward Him would be creative or expressed in different ways as well.

In chapter 5, I mentioned just how often the words "praise" and "worship" appear in the Bible. But what I didn't mention was that the original, biblical texts used a myriad of different words to describe different expressions of praise and worship. This is why it is so important that, when studying the Bible, we make an effort to find the original words, whether they be in Hebrew, Greek, or Aramaic, to get the full understanding of whatever text or subject we are studying. The biblical authors clearly made distinctions when it came to praise and worship because they knew that there wasn't just a "one-size-fits-all" approach. Different people in different circumstances expressed their praise/worship in different ways.

Being raised Pentecostal, the type of praise and worship I was (and am) accustomed to is that loud, expressive, almost fanatical type of praise. It's the type of shouting and yelling that most people only experience whenever they go to a sports game or a rock concert. I remember vividly how I once went to one of the college football bowl games with my brother. I was sitting literally two inches away from him and the crowd was so loud that when he would try to say something to me, I could barely hear him. I'm sure I must've been thinking, *I feel like I'm in one of our church services!* Pretty sure some of you can also relate.

Now, a lot of people have an issue with this. For the type of people that are more introverted or more "relaxed," so to speak, they question why some church services have to be so loud and expressive. Because, let's face it, many people would prefer to simply come to church, sit down, not say anything, listen to the Word, and go home. Almost like a spiritual "drive- through"; get in and get out without doing anything besides pulling up.

But the problem is that the people who are that way, never experience the full measure of God's presence over their lives. Why? Simple. Psalm 22:3 tells us that:

"...O thou that inhabits the praises of Israel."

"Inhabits" the praises... The word "inhabits" means "to live in or occupy a place." King David is letting us know through this psalm that God "lives in" praise. He manifests Himself during praise. When you praise Him, you begin to see Him. When you praise Him, He begins to break chains in your family. When you praise God, His presence begins to move! This should be motivation enough for you to put this book down for the next few moments and just begin to give God praise wherever you may be, knowing that while you praise Him, changes begin to take place!

Now, David uses the Hebrew word "Tehillah" in this verse. Tehillah can be translated as "laudation" or more simply as "praises." This is a word most people probably haven't heard of since their English class in high school. Laudation comes from the Latin word "laudere," which means "to praise someone extravagantly (there's that word again), usually in a very public manner." Laudation also refers to praising someone or something through singing.

So, as you can see, when David tells us that God inhabits (lives in) the praises of His people, he is referring to praise done through singing and/or through a very public expression. That is why I tell people that church is not for spectators, i.e., it's not for people who want to just sit and "enjoy the show." It is not a place for people who simply want to ease their religious conscience by attending Sunday morning service. It is for people who have a desire to express their praises publicly with their brothers and sisters in Christ. It is a place where those of us who have been redeemed by the blood of the Lamb can unite and express our gratitude and admiration toward God!

Now, if you have been to church, it's likely that within the first thirty seconds of being there, you've heard someone shout "Hallelujah!" Whether it's while they are praying, while the worship team is at the altar, or when someone is preaching, there is always at least that ONE loud person shouting Hallelujah so loud, even the people in the parking lot can hear them! This word is something people say customarily without truly understanding its meaning. It's almost just "something we say" in church because it's a word we've heard on a regular basis.

Interestingly enough, however, the word "Hallelujah" is actually a composite of two different Hebrew words. The first is "Halal" and the second is "Yah," which is a shortened version of God's name, Yahweh. Hallelujah simply means "praise the Lord," but again, what kind or expression of praise does it refer to? Well, "Halal" means a few things. It means:

1. To boast/be boastful.
2. To be clamorously foolish.
3. To rave or celebrate.

All these meanings have one thing in common: They all refer to the type of praise that is loud and excessive. It is the type of praise that makes you sweat, jump, run, yell, and makes you look like you are going insane! That's why I specifically like that the word means to be clamorously foolish, because a lot of us are used to the pretty, little services where everyone is in their own corner just minding their business, not saying much and not doing much. Truly praising God is not pretty or cute. It can be messy. It can be, dare I say, ugly. It can even be annoying to people that have not encountered God on a deep level.

Remember when I spoke about Kind David worshipping God with all his might when he and the Israelites recovered the Ark of the Covenant from the home of Obed-Edom? See, the interesting thing about that story happened once they entered Jerusalem. David, being a man after God's own heart, simply cared about paying homage to the God he served and loved. The Bible tells us that David stripped down to a loincloth and began to jump and shout and dance before the Lord. Unbeknown to him, however, his wife was looking at him from afar.

As the ark of the LORD came into the city of David, Michal the daughter of Saul looked out of the window and saw King David leaping and dancing before the LORD, and she despised him in her heart.

— 2 SAMUEL 6:16

David was minding his own business, praising the Lord, yet his wife was looking at him with disgust. She despised him for praising God. I don't know about you, but this is a concept I've had difficulty trying to get my head around. How can you *despise* someone simply based on the way they praise God? How can anyone hate someone or feel contempt toward someone all because they choose to praise God in the way He deserves to be praised? There is a phrase I love to say when I get up to preach, and it is this:

"If you don't know what I've been through, you have no right to criticize my worship!"

READ and re-read this statement until it gets down into your spirit. Post it on your Facebook, your Instagram, make a poster and put it on your bedroom door, etc. Do whatever you have to do but never forget that phrase. No one, and I mean **NO ONE,** has the right to judge you based on how "extra" you are when it comes to praising God. No one can tell you that you are "being too loud" or that you are being obnoxious. Because, frankly, Halal praise *is* obnoxious. It *is* annoying. Halal praise makes anyone that is not spiritual look at you in disgust the same way Michal was looking at David from her window.

And David returned to bless his household. But Michal the daughter of Saul came out to meet David and said, "How the king of Israel honored himself today, uncovering himself today before the eyes of his servants' female servants, as one of the vulgar fellows shamelessly uncovers himself!" And David said to Michal, "It was before the LORD, who chose me above your father and above all his house, to appoint me as prince over Israel, the people of the LORD—and I will celebrate before the LORD. I will make myself yet more contemptible than this, and I will be abased in your eyes. But by the female servants of whom you have spoken, by them I shall be held in honor." And Michal the daughter of Saul had no child to the day of her death.

— 2 SAMUEL 6: 20-23

David, the king of Israel and the king of the clap backs too! Michal basically told David, "How *dare* you praise God that way, seeing that you are the king of Israel?!" His response, in other words, was, "If you think the way I'm praising is bad now, you ain't seen nothing yet!" If that's not the heart of a worshiper, I don't know what is. He told his own wife that he basically didn't care if he looked ridiculous; he was praising God! And due to Michal's criticism of the way David was praising, the text tells us that she was barren from that moment forward. Her barrenness was God's judgement over her life, all because she dared to despise her husband because he praised God in a way she deemed "dishonorable."

It is my sincere hope and prayer that the next time we find someone else's praise appalling and despicable, we think twice before saying anything, because God obviously doesn't take too kindly to the criticism of those who refuse to praise and worship

Him in the way He deserves. He isn't interested in hearing the murmurs and complaints of people that judge others based on how they express themselves in worship. You want a deeper relationship with God? Forget about everybody else and focus on truly praising Him in a way that invites His presence to manifest. Because God LIVES in the praises of His people!

8

A PRAISE FOR VICTORY

"And when they began to sing and praise, the LORD set Pan ambush against the men of Ammon, Moab, and Mount Seir, who had come against Judah, so that they were routed."

— 2 CHRONICLES 20:22

Something most people don't know is that my life has been one full of doctors' appointments, X-rays, MRIs, physical therapies, and surgeries. Part of my testimony is that I was born with what is medically called "bilateral hip dysplasia." In layman's terms, I was born with both my hips dislocated, four inches above where a normal hip should be, and I was also missing the acetabulum, better known as the hip joint. Not only that, but my left elbow was dislocated as well. When I was around six months old, my parents noticed my feet started pointing outward and that I couldn't walk on my own without falling to the ground shortly after.

That is when they decided to take me to specialists in Puerto Rico. After some examinations, my parents received word from the doctor that would change their lives forever. Due to my condition, they were told I was never going to walk, run, grow, or be a "normal" child. The only option they were given was to send me to Philadelphia order to operate on my hips. Post-surgery, I was supposed to stay for six months in recovery, being monitored by doctors and physical therapists. So, my family made all the arrangements and raised the funds necessary so my mother and I could go, with the hope of me being somehow cured.

We left from San Juan, Puerto Rico and arrived at Shriners Hospital for Children in Philadelphia, Pennsylvania. My mother and I went through the pre-surgery protocols, anxiously antici-pating the day of the surgery. We spent about two weeks in the hospital before I was set for my procedure. My mother has almost two boxes full of pictures showcasing our journey. Till this day, when I see them, it's hard not to get teary eyed. Once the day of surgery arrived, they took me away because the head surgeon wanted to examine some X-rays of my hips to make sure everything was still the same. Mom was in the waiting room when, again, more bad news arrived.

The surgeon walked into the waiting room and said, "I'm sorry, Mrs. Santiago. We cannot perform the surgery on him. If we do, he will simply be confined to a wheelchair the rest of his life." Mom told me she broke down because she couldn't believe she flew all this way, alone, barely knowing a word of English, to simply be told that there was nothing that could be done for me. Imagine the emotions she was going through at that moment. She said she began to argue with the doctor but his answer simply was, "If you want, we can operate. But he will be in a wheelchair. Your choice."

Out of options, we both got on a flight back to Puerto Rico and my mother was seemingly destroyed. Her emotions were all over the place while her mind wandered toward what was to become of her two-year-old son sitting next to her. As the plane was arriving in Puerto Rico, she said she had a strange experience. She began to hear the voice of the enemy telling her repeatedly, "You are defeated."

See, one thing the enemy loves to do is kick someone while they are already down. My mother was distraught at the situation, and the enemy took full advantage to bring her down even further. "You are defeated" this demonic voice kept repeating to her. However, during this experience, my mother lifted her head toward heaven and said the following words:

"God, if you heal him, you are God. But if you DON'T heal him, you are STILL God!"

See, Mom knew that her praise and worship was not dependent on external circumstances. She was going through an emotional rollercoaster while the enemy was whispering in her ear, and she STILL chose to praise God *while on an airplane!* My beloved brother/sister, it is very easy to praise God when things are going your way. It is easy to go to church and worship God when you have money in your bank account, when your marriage is stable, when your kids love you, and when you have your health in check. It is easy to lift your hands and say, "God is good" when you seem "too blessed to be stressed." But how many of us, like Momma, can lift our hands, look to heaven, and chose to praise Him while hell itself is trying to destroy you? It's one thing to praise Him in the promised land, but can you worship Him in the desert?

The reason I'm telling you all this is because many people do not understand that sometimes, the secret to our victory is found in your ability to praise Him in the storm. Most people wait until

AFTER the battle is over to praise God. Most people wait until their situation is resolved to magnify the name of God. We have been taught to P.U.S.H. (Pray Until Something Happens) when things get tough but have not been told we also need to praise until something happens.

In 2 Chronicles 20, Israel finds itself in an extremely dire situation. The Moabites, Ammonites, and the Meunites had marched their way from their homelands in order to take over and subdue Israel.

Some men came and told Jehoshaphat, "A great multitude is coming against you from Edom."

— *2 CHRONICLES 20:2*

Seemingly facing destruction, fear overtook King Jehoshaphat and he proclaimed a nationwide fast to ask the Lord what they must do to avoid certain annihilation. All of Judah fasted, prayed, and humbled themselves until the Lord answered them. As they prayed, verse 14 tells us that the Spirit of the Lord fell upon one of the Levites, Jahaziel, and he began to declare the prophetic utterance. The Lord answered the Jews by telling them three main things:

1. Do not be afraid.
2. Stand firm.
3. See the salvation of the Lord.

Let me stop here for just a moment and declare a prophetic word over your life. It is possible that you might be facing opposition right now. Possibly, like the Jews, the enemy has encamped around your house, your family, and your ministry, threatening to destroy you. But the Lord tells you today, "Do not be afraid! This battle is not yours. This battle is mine. Stand firm and see what I am about to do!" Don't worry about the when and the how. If He said He is going to do it, He will fulfill that which He has promised!

God told them, "This one is mine," yet they still had to go out to the battlefield. They couldn't just stay in their homes. They still to go out to where the enemy was. However, the Bible tells us that King Jehoshaphat rose early in the morning, not just with his army but with the Levites. If there were a group of people that did not belong on the battlefield, it was the Levites. As a matter of fact, in the book of Numbers, God specifically told Moses to withhold the names of the Levites from the list of men who could serve in the army. God did not call them to be warriors; they were priests. Yet in almost every major battle the Jews fought, the Levites were present.

The Levites were responsible for serving in the tabernacle and, later, the temple. They were responsible for carrying the Ark of the Covenant any time it needed to be moved. And many Levites were also singers and musicians that were tasked with leading praise and worship everywhere they were! In other words, they were the original worship teams of their day! We will talk a bit more about the Levites soon but for now, it should suffice to know that Levites, aka the worship leaders, were present in this battle.

The king knew he wasn't going to fight this battle through traditional means. In fact, he wasn't going to fight this battle *at all*. Yet he brough the Levites knowing that if they can praise God while facing their enemies, God would surely give them the victory, just as He promised! And surely enough, verse 22 tell us that "as they began to sing and praise," God began fighting on their behalf. Can you imagine being in the opposite army, seeing the Jews from a distance and instead of seeing them ready to launch an attack, you hear them singing and praising the Lord? And as they praised, God suddenly showed up and started fighting for them. That must've been one incredible scene!

You might be wondering what this has to do with my mother and I. Well, at the time, my mom didn't realize it but that small act of praise and worship was the key that unlocked her victory. One week after we arrived back to the island, there was an evangelistic service in our local church. Coincidentally, or better said by divine purpose, the guest preacher of the night was an ex-medical student whom God called to be a full-time evangelist. Even though I was just over two years old at the time, I remember that night vividly as if it happened yesterday. The preacher made the altar call and most of the church passes to the altar. I was in the very back row with my mom, and I said, "Mommy, Mommy, up there! Take me up there. Pray, Mommy, pray," while I was laying my hand on my head to let her know I wanted them to pray for me.

So, she did. She picked me up and carried me to the altar (since I still couldn't walk more than a couple steps by myself) and stood in front of the preacher. He asked her what was wrong, and she proceeded to explain about my condition. He stopped her in the middle of her explanation because, as an ex-medical student, he knew what she was referring to. He proceeded to lay hands on my hips as I was still being carried by my mother. Everyone in the church was standing in agreement in prayer. He told her to lay me down, believing that the miracle was already done, looked at me, and told me to "walk from here to here."

Suddenly, the little two-year-old boy who had never taken more than two or three steps without falling face-first to the ground now began to run around the church! It's obvious to say that the everyone within the church erupted in praise because everyone knew my story. For weeks onward, my father would always ask my mother if I had fallen during the day, which she would happily respond "no!" God is still a God of miracles! When man says something is impossible, God says "Oh yea? Watch this."

Just one week before, my mother was unsure of her son's future. Yet now, her son was walking and running like any other child. Just like God gave the Israelites the victory during their praise, so God gave my mother the miracle she was longing for all ... preceded by a single act of praise. And if He did it with us, He can do it for you! You want to see God fight your battles? Then praise Him!

9

THE WORSHIPPING BRIDE

"I am my beloved's, and my beloved is mine..."

— SONG OF SOLOMON 6: 3

I f you were to ask people what the most beautiful book in the Bible is, chances are they would say "Psalms." The poetic nature of the book of Psalms gives us a little bit of everything. They show us moments of deep, emotional anguish, moments of thanksgiving, moments of fear, moments of repentances, moments of admiration, and much more. I've stated many times in different Bible studies and preaching that if someone wants to truly learn how to pray, read Psalms. I promise your prayer life will dramatically change!

Having said that, however, I believe the most beautiful book in the Bible is not Psalms, but Song of Songs. Written by King Solomon around 965 BC, it tells the tale of a young shepherd (possibly Solomon) and a Shulamite woman. This book paints a perfect picture of a young couple who are madly in love, expressing their affection and desire for one another. From the pre-marital stage to the wedding/honeymoon stage and, ultimately, the mature marriage phase, we see their romance grow into something truly remarkable.

Unlike most books in the Bible, this book is explicit in nature. The young man and the Shulamite are very detailed in their description of one another and in their desire for each other. Some people even believed it shouldn't be a part of the Bible because of its sexual undertones! Yet God gave us this book for us to know what true love between a husband and wife looks like and what He intended as far as sex. Because F.Y.I., sex is not "gross" or "taboo," but was created BY GOD for the enjoyment of a husband and wife! But I'll write a book about that another time.

Most people just take Song of Songs as just that, a book about sex and marriage. Yet, like with all things in the Bible, there's more to it than meets the eye. (I channeled my inner Optimus Prime for that sentence. I regret nothing.) The Bible teaches us that the things found in the Old Testament/the law of Moses were a shadow of things to come. In other words, they were a prototype or, a "rough draft" if you will, of things that were to take place in the New Covenant established by the death and resurrection of Jesus. Let's take the wilderness tabernacle, for example.

The entrance, the sacrificial altar, the candelabrum, the veil, the Holy of Holies, the Ark of the Covenant, the mercy seat, etc.: All those things were different pictures of the work of Christ. The veil was symbolic of the separation between God and man due to sin. Then when Jesus died on the cross, the veil was torn, symbolizing that we now had full access into the presence of God. The sacrificial altar was symbolic of Jesus being sacrificed as the Lamb of God. The high priest was symbolic of Jesus being our high priest, our mediator to God, and so on.

Not only that, but different people in the Old Testament were types of the coming Messiah. Adam was a type of Christ. Joseph was a type of Christ. Moses, Jonah, Melchizedek, and many more figures can, in one form or another, relate to Jesus and His works. These were all shadows of what was to be in the future. So if that is the case, with all those examples I gave above, why would the Shulamite and the young shepherd be any different? There must be some sort of parallel, however minute it might be, that will lead us closer to Christ.

Near the end of Ephesians 5, the apostle Paul gave marital advice to wives and husbands. He told us that the wife was supposed to submit to the husband, being that the husband was the head of the wife as Christ was the head of the church. He then went on to say that the husband was to love his wife in the same way that Christ loved the church, laying down His life for her. Then, in Revelation 19:7, we read:

"Let us rejoice and exult and give him the glory, for the marriage of the Lamb has come, and his Bride has made herself ready."

The "bride" that is mentioned here is not a human bride but is the church. Those of us that have been redeemed by the blood of the Lamb (Jesus) are part of the *ekklesia*, which is why we are called the Bride of Christ.

With that being said, I am of the sort who believe deeply that Song of Songs is not *just* a book about romance between a man and a woman, but it can be used as a sort of parable to give us an insight into what the relationship the bride (church) and the bridegroom (Jesus) are supposed to have. Jesus obviously loves His bride with a perfect, unending love. He cares for her, protects her, covers her, looks out for her, and wants nothing but the very best for her. But how are we as the church, the bride of Christ, to love our Bridegroom?

When we open the Bible to read Song of Songs, almost right away we see how the Shulamite felt about her betrothed. The way she expresses and describes the love toward him and how he made her feel, one could almost say that she was obsessed! In chapter 2 verse 5, she says that she was "sick with love." Now, before I go on, I want you to do me a favor. I want you to remember the time where you first fell in love. Think of the butterflies you felt with the mere thought of that significant other. Think of how you would write poems for her at three in the morning or how you would write down his name over and over and over again in your notebook because you couldn't imagine a day where even his name wouldn't cross your mind!

Recently, I got married to the most amazing, beautiful, smart, selfless woman of God I've ever met. She is the love of my life and is truly a blessing from God to have her in my life. As her husband, my goals are to love her, cherish her, and make her the happiest woman alive. There is nothing I wouldn't do for her to make her smile. There is nothing I wouldn't do to please her and show her how much her husband loves, cherishes, and appreciates her. Why? Because I'm in love with her! Because I made a commitment to be hers and only hers until the day Jesus comes back or He calls me home!

Now, the same way each and every one of us would do absolutely anything for the man or woman we love; the same way many of you stepped on an altar and said "I do" and committed your life to loving your spouse; the same way we would climb mountains, cross rivers, and travel through deserts in order to do what needs to be done for our spouses; is the same way the church, the glorious Bride of Christ, should feel and act like toward their beloved Jesus. The same way many of you can't go a day or two without seeing your significant other is the same way we should feel whenever we spend any amount of time away from His presence.

Over and over, the Shulamite expressed how she longed for her beloved. She couldn't stand to be away from him. She couldn't bear the thought of her beloved being gone for long. She wanted him to stay with her and wanted to give him all her love and give herself up to him continually. She was mad with love and was overcome with desire for him. In many ways, she almost *worshipped* him and the ground he walked on because in her eyes, there was nothing greater on this earth than the arms of her beloved and she would do anything for him.

That is the way we are to be with Jesus. We should long for His presence all the days of our lives. We should feel "lovesick" for Him. We should have that initiative to do whatever we need to do to do His will. Too many of us go to church not out of love, but out of routine. Too many of us preach and sing and do ministry simply because we think it's "the right thing" to do; not from a place of true desire to please Him but a place of religious contentment. We should praise and worship Him from a place of deep desire and affection, not to give what we want. (I know that one hurt a lot of you. If it did, just say "ouch".)

In Revelation 2, we read the words Jesus was speaking to the church in Ephesus. He complimented them on their patience, endurance, the works they did, the intolerance to false apostles, and those who do evil. Yet, in verse 4, He said something that should shake many to the core: "I have this against you, that you have abandoned your first love." In the following verse, He goes on to tell them to repent. This is a church that had it all: good teachers, preachers; they did mighty works; they were steadfast; they did not tolerate those who proclaimed to be something they were not and so on. In many respects, this was the model of the ideal church! The church of Ephesus should've been the poster boy for churches. YET! Jesus scolded them because they did all these things but still had abandoned their love for Him.

Church became routine. Worship became monotonous. Prayer was simply a religious rite. Everything was dull. They did many great things... but forgot the thing that mattered the most: their love for their Beloved. Many people tend to forget that being a Christian and being the bride is more than ministry. It's more than holding a microphone on Sunday mornings. It's more than attending your local church services every day of the week. It is about the relationship you have with Jesus. It is about what you do when there is no service and there is no preaching and there is no evangelism. Do you desire Him daily, or do you desire Him only on Sundays?

I can tell you this much: God does not want a part-time hook-up. He is not interested in having half your time and half of your attention. He is not looking for something mediocre. He is not looking for a "one night stand." He is looking for a full-time bride that will love Him, adore Him, worship Him, acknowledge Him, and long to be with Him all the days of her life!

10

BRING ME A MINSTREL

"But now bring me a minstrel. And it came to pass, when the minstrel played, that the hand of the LORD came upon him."

— 2 KINGS 3:15

When we gather in our weekly church service, most of the time what is emphasized the most is, obviously, the preaching. After all, what would church be without good, sound preaching delivered by an excellent communicator? We can never expect to grow in our faith unless we have someone properly teaching us the Word of God and guiding us as we travel down this road called Christianity. Now, as important as sound preaching is, one thing that I cannot stress enough is the importance of minstrels within the body of Christ. What is a minstrel? I'm glad you asked!

The first time we run into the word "minstrel" in the Bible, if you are using the King James Version, is found in 2 Kings 3:15.

In its simplest definition, the word "minstrel" means "a singer and/or a player of stringed-instruments." Think of King David who, before becoming king, would play the harp before King Saul and the tormenting spirits would depart from him. Known as the sweet Psalmist of Israel, David wrote seventy-three psalms that were meant to be sung and accompanied by all kinds of musical instruments. There is even a story in 1 Chronicles 15 that tells us David instructed the Levites to appoint musicians and singers to play and sing as they took the Ark of the Covenant back to Jerusalem. He knew just how important it was not just to worship with our lips or our lifestyles, but with music! Even before David died, he had assigned 288 musicians and 24 different choral groups to lead the praise and worship in what would later be called Solomon's Temple!

Can you imagine the amazing sound that would come from the Temple as you walked toward it to present your sacrifices and offerings to God? It surely must've been a sight and a sound to behold. Even during the dedication ceremony of the Temple, once the Levites had placed the Ark of the Covenant in the Holy of Holies, there were 120 Levitical musicians playing silver trumpets, as well as many others who were playing harps, cymbals and lyres. Oh! And this doesn't even include the 4,000 musicians/singers David had appointed right before he died. It's safe to say how important music was to the ancient Israelites.

Now, these musicians that were appointed for the Temple were not just any old musicians. I'm not just talking about someone who can play two or three chords on the piano or guitar. I'm talking about musicians who were truly skilled at what they did and dedicated their lives to the mastery of their craft. First Chronicles 9:33 tells us that these musicians were "free from any other work." What does that mean? Simple. It meant that all they devoted their time and efforts to was music. It wasn't their part-time jobs or side gigs they did on the weekends. Music, by all accounts, WAS THEIR LIVES!

Why were they free from other work? Because David knew that if you are going to play for God, you must play in excellence! David knew how important it was to have SKILLED musicians who were dedicated to the Lord, and he knew they couldn't play as well as they should if their energy, thoughts, and desires were split between other tasks.

Now, let's get one thing out of the way: The God we serve deserves excellence. Many people justify giving God less than what He deserves all because "God knows my heart." Way too often have I seen and heard people get up on an altar, grab a microphone, and say things along the lines of "I don't sing well but God knows my heart. I don't play well but God knows my heart. I'm not the best preacher but God knows my heart." Usually, what follows those words is a lackluster performance that makes those in attendance beg for the torture to stop. It sounds harsh but it is the truth. We have become so accustomed to mundane routines that we are satisfied with giving God the bare minimum. We give God and God's people "good enough" to just get by, but not "good enough" to transform and impact lives on a deeper level.

I wonder how different our weekly church services would be if we had more musicians that were as dedicated to God and as dedicated to their craft as these Levites were. I wonder what kind of impact the church would have if we would invest as much in our musicians and singers as we do in our preachers and pastors. If excellence in praise and worship was a requirement and was the standard, not the exception, the glory of God would invade every single church gathering like never before! Now, back to the story in 2 Kings.

Truth be told, this is one of my favorite Bible stories: 1) because it's easy to follow; and 2) because it has some hidden gems. Here, we find the Moabites rebelling against the Israelites instead of paying their tribute of 100,000 lambs and rams. The Moabite king mustered his armies and marched toward Israel. Jehoram, the king of Israel at the time, called up the king of Edom and Jehoshaphat, king of Judah, to help him fight the Moabites. After the three armies marched around for seven days, they could not find any water and were on the verge of perishing. So, King Jehoshaphat asked if there was a prophet around so they might "inquire of the Lord" (2 Kings 3:11). Lo and behold, the prophet Elisha was in the area. The three kings went down to where Elisha was, hoping to receive a word of guidance or assurance of the Lord.

Now, the fact that Elisha was a prophet cannot be emphasized enough. Prophets are people connected to God on a much deeper level. Prophets are men and women who, in a sense, have their ears bound to the mouth of God. They speak the oracles of God. They can see, hear, smell, taste, and touch things that the average person could not, simply because of how spiritually sensitive they are...and the three kings knew this. But something interesting happened during this meeting. Elisha...the prophet of God...did not immediately receive a word from God concerning their situation. He didn't even so much as want to see them if it were not for the fact that he respected King Jehoshaphat.

In fact, Elisha was so upset at the king of Israel because he did evil in the sight of God that in verse 13, he basically told King Jehoram that instead of coming to him, he should've just gone instead to the false prophets of the gods his mother and father worshipped. So, Elisha made a seemingly small request... "bring me a minstrel" (verse 15). He asked the kings to bring him a musician, a person skilled in playing the harp/stringed instruments. The interesting thing about this whole thing is that Elisha did not receive a word from God until the minstrel played! My God, I'm about to shout! I got to say that one more time.

ELISHA DID NOT RECEIVE A WORD FROM GOD UNTIL THE MINSTREL PLAYED!

Clearly, Elisha knew how important an anointed and gifted musician was in this scenario. The Moabites were in open rebellion, threatening the Israelites. You have an evil king, a pagan king, and a godly king asking God for help because they were perishing. On top of that, you have an angry, zealous prophet who didn't even want to look at them except Jehoshaphat. So, he needed someone who would open the heavens on his behalf. He needed someone to get him in tune with the spirit of God to be in the proper position to hear what God was saying. So, he called for a minstrel!

We must get to a place in God where we fully understand that the true secret to having the glory of God descend in our services, the secret to accessing the supernatural, the secret to hearing the word of the Lord, is found when we have anointed minstrels in our midst who are so in tune with the Spirit that they can play the sounds of heaven here on Earth. Minstrels, musicians, hear me out. You must understand that not everyone that comes to service has the desire to worship. People come to church stressed out, frustrated, sick, tired, annoyed, angry. They come with a whole lot of baggage and, often, they will have difficulty getting into the Holy of Holies.

But believe me when I tell you, there is something that happens, something that shifts in the spirit, when a musician who is in tune with God and is skillful in what they do begins to play. When you, Minstrel, begin to worship through your music, you are "unlocking the heavens," so to speak. You are engaging in spiritual warfare on behalf of your brother and sister that came to church all kinds of messed up. You are the key for God's people to receive His glory! There have been times where I wasn't able to properly preach until there was a minstrel playing. There are times I am not able to prophesize unless a minstrel is playing.

There are times I cannot focus on my assignment in God unless there is music being played that will help me tap into the presence of God.

Do not let anyone devalue the calling and assignment of the minstrel, because often the secret to our healing and deliverance is found in their worship!

11

FINAL WORDS

"Bless the LORD, O my soul: and all that is within me, bless his holy name"

— PSALM 103:1

I believe this is the time where the Lord is making an invitation. God is inviting every one of us to enter deeper levels of fellowship and intimacy with Him through worship. There are many of you who God is going to raise up to change and transform cities, regions, even nations. Many of you, God is going to raise up as prophetic voices within the government, just like Daniel. Many of you, God is going to raise up with powerful healing and deliverance ministries. There is a lot of hurt within the body of Christ. There are many wounded and sick people, and this is the generation that will usher in the next and final move of God on the earth. But all of this will be made possible only by those who accept this invitation to worship God like they never had before. Because only worshippers who worship in spirit and in truth will have the capacity to carry the glory of God!

This is your time, beloved reader. This is your season! Rise up in Jesus's name! Accept His invitation and I promise, you will begin to see the power of God manifesting in your life like never before!

ACKNOWLEDGMENTS

First and foremost, I would like to thank the godfather of ghostwriting himself, Eli "Che" Gonzalez. We met a decade ago and I cannot describe the impact you have had on my life. From that first conversation we had when I was 18, driving down the road to pick up some KFC to you now, almost 10 years later, publishing my first book, my gratitude towards you is indescribable. I truly look up to you and even though I am almost 28 now, I want to be like you when I grow up ha-ha! Secondly, to everyone at "The Ghost Publishing." You guys made my childhood dream come true. I will be eternally grateful and I'm looking forward to working on more books with this company! Third, to my beautiful Momma Bear, Maria Gonzalez. Thank you for believing me and for always giving me words of encouragement. They have been a balm to my heart in difficult times. Fourth, to my Pastor, Wilfredo Rosado and everyone at the most amazing church in all of Florida, H2 Christian Church! If you look up "model church" in the dictionary, there would be a picture of all you guys there. Pastor Wilfredo, you're the best pastor anyone could ask for. Thank you for your support, prayers, encouragement, corrections and care. Also, I'd like to thank he BEST photographer ever, my older brother Joshua for the videos and photoshoots. You are the GOAT. And lastly, I would like to thank my friends Marc, Beatriz, Jay, Jireh, Isaiah, Eddy, Laci, as well as my brother-in-law, Bryan, for loving and believing in me. I'm blessed to have you all as my friends

ABOUT THE AUTHOR

Jose Santiago is a sought-after preacher, teacher and conference speaker that has been in ministry for 12 years. He is the founder of "Voice That Cries Out Prophetic Ministries" which is a ministry dedicated to impacting the world through the power of the Holy Ghost. Every weekend, you can find him preaching in different churches across the country. When he is not traveling however, he is at home with his beautiful wife Kimberly Santiago and their three kids: Jack, Kianna, and baby A.J. He is also a member of H2 Christian Church in Orlando, FL, pastored by Wilfredo Rosado.

To book Jose for your next revival, conference, camp, or service, call 813-389-6142 or send an e-mail to santiagojose1537@gmail.com and leave a detailed message stating your name, church/organization's name, dates, time, and address of the event, and you will receive a call back as soon as possible.